As You Were

A farce by
Johann Nestroy

Translated from the German and adapted by
Geoffrey Skelton

Samuel French—London
New York-Toronto-Hollywood

© 1997 BY GEOFFREY SKELTON

Rights of Performance by Amateurs are controlled by Samuel French Ltd, 52 Fitzroy Street, London W1P 6JR, and they, or their authorized agents, issue licences to amateurs on payment of a fee. **It is an infringement of the Copyright to give any performance or public reading of the play before the fee has been paid and the licence issued.**

The Royalty Fee indicated below is subject to contract and subject to variation at the sole discretion of Samuel French Ltd.

    Basic fee for each and every
      performance by amateurs   Code D
    in the British Isles

The Professional Rights in this play are controlled by DAVID HIGHAM ASSOCIATES LIMITED 5-8 Lower John Street, Golden Square, London W1R 4HA.

The publication of this play does not imply that it is necessarily available for performance by amateurs or professionals, either in the British Isles or Overseas. Amateurs and professionals considering a production are strongly advised in their own interests to apply to the appropriate agents for consent before starting rehearsals or booking a theatre or hall.

ISBN 0 573 12138 9

Please see page iv for further copyright information

LINCOLNSHIRE
COUNTY COUNCIL

822

CHARACTERS

Michael Hofmann, a rich timber merchant
Helena, his wife
Josie, the new maidservant
Muffett, the new manservant

Setting — An elegant living-room
Time — Mid-nineteenth century*

* Although originally mid-nineteenth century, the play could be staged in any setting from mid-nineteenth to mid-twentieth century. Consequently salary references on page 8 may be altered at the director's discretion.

COPYRIGHT INFORMATION
(See also page ii)

This play is fully protected under the Copyright Laws of the British Commonwealth of Nations, the United States of America and all countries of the Berne and Universal Copyright Conventions.

All rights, including Stage, Motion Picture, Radio, Television, Public Reading, and Translation into Foreign Languages, are strictly reserved.

No part of this publication may lawfully be reproduced in ANY form or by any means — photocopying, typescript, recording (including video-recording), manuscript, electronic, mechanical, or otherwise — or be transmitted or stored in a retrieval system, without prior permission.

Licences are issued subject to the understanding that it shall be made clear in all advertising matter that the audience will witness an amateur performance; that the names of the authors of the plays shall be included on all announcements and on all programmes; and that the integrity of the authors' work will be preserved.

The Royalty Fee is subject to contract and subject to variation at the sole discretion of Samuel French Ltd.

In Theatres or Halls seating Four Hundred or more the fee will be subject to negotiation.

In Territories Overseas the fee quoted in this Acting Edition may not apply. A fee will be quoted on application to our local authorized agent, or if there is no such agent, on application to Samuel French Ltd, London.

VIDEO-RECORDING OF AMATEUR PRODUCTIONS

Please note that the copyright laws governing video-recording are extremely complex and that it should not be assumed that any play may be video-recorded for *whatever purpose* without first obtaining the permission of the appropriate agents. The fact that a play is published by Samuel French Ltd does not indicate that video rights are available or that Samuel French Ltd controls such rights.

TRANSLATOR'S NOTE

The Austrian actor-manager Johann Nestroy (1801-1862) was one of the leading figures of the nineteenth-century Viennese Volkstheater (People's Theatre), and many of his eighty-odd plays are still widely performed in Germany and Austria. In them he pokes good-humoured fun at human behaviour from the viewpoint of the humbler social classes for which the Volkstheater catered.

As You Were (Frühere Verhältnisse) was one of Nestroy's last plays, and was first performed in 1862, the year of his death. He played the part of Muffett.

AS YOU WERE

An elegant living-room with doors at centre and both sides

Michael Hofmann enters R, followed by his wife Helena. He is in a dressing-gown, she in negligée

Hofmann But dearest wife, sweetest of sweethearts, you can't blame that on me.
Helena Not a single servant in the house, and it's all your fault. You've even thrown out your own manservant.
Hofmann He was stealing my cigars.
Helena A few paltry cigars. As if that mattered!
Hofmann My cigars are not paltry. In fact, they're enormous, particularly the cost. And in any case we wouldn't be in this position if you hadn't insisted on packing off your chambermaid. And why? Just because ——
Helena —— I saw you stroking her cheeks.
Hofmann I? When?
Helena Never mind when — I saw it.
Hofmann Why must women always judge things by what they see? A casual movement of the hand, a servant's cheek happening, while dusting, to brush lightly against it: why should that make you jump to conclusions?
Helena It wasn't the first time. You are always over-familiar with the servants.
Hofmann I treat them all exactly the same. Well — almost.
Helena And what have you done about getting replacements?
Hofmann I've put a card in the greengrocer's window.
Helena The greengrocer's window! Why will you persist in following that unutterably vulgar practice?
Hofmann He's a very respectable greengrocer.

Helena Oh, stop it! Who would ever think you're the son-in-law of a professor? If my poor father had lived to see what a common man you are!

Hofmann I must say, my angel, you are a very disagreeable angel this morning.

Helena I am not an angel yet, but still the daughter of a very eminent professor, used all my life to the comforts of a well-run household. If, within half an hour from now, I am not provided with a maidservant, I shall leave you and go to my aunt's. Oh, my dear father, why did you have to die?

Hofmann You make it sound as if that's my fault too. As far as I'm concerned, he could have gone on being a professor till kingdom come.

Helena That's quite enough. I give you thirty minutes — at the outside — to find a maid for me. You had better start at once. You have no time to lose.

Helena exits L

Hofmann Wonderful woman, my wife — good-looking, young, striking personality — but I must admit, I feel easier when she's not there. It's not that I don't care for her. On the contrary, I adore her. But if only she'd stop harking on her good family! It embarrasses me, it goads me into trying to score off her. There's nothing worse than having always to look up to your own wife. It gives you a sort of moral crick in your neck. If my darling professor's daughter knew that my parents kept a shoe shop, and that I myself — (*looking round as if in fear of being heard*) — I hope no-one's listening! — was once a gentleman's gentleman. Well, that's how it was, and the worst thing about what was is that it's always likely to catch up with what is. Now I'd better get dressed and visit that domestic agency. Half an hour, she said, or it's goodbye to my well-bred angel.

Hofmann goes off R. *The stage is empty for a moment. Then there is a knock at the door* C

As You Were

Helena comes in L and goes to door C

Helena So this is what it has come to — I have to answer my own door now!

Helena opens door C to disclose Josie, who is wearing elegant but worn clothing

Yes? What is it?

Josie Miss Helena, ma'am, have you forgotten me?

Helena Josie, is it you? After all these years!

Josie Josie Amsel it is, your ladyship. Formerly cook to your late father, the professor, and now a member of the theatrical profession.

Helena You, an actress, Josie? Come in, come in. How exciting!

Josie (*entering*) Yes, ma'am, I exchanged the kitchen stove for the boards — the worst day's work I ever did, if the truth be known.

Helena You were unsuccessful?

Josie Oh, I had my successes all right. Joan of Arc — I could do the maid a treat. And my Ophelia — there's rosemary, that's for remembrance — never a dry eye in the house.

Helena But that is splendid! Then why ——?

Josie The theatres I played in didn't have the habit of paying salaries, and they wouldn't change their ways for me. I never had the good fortune to get engaged in the sort of theatre that has a millionaire in every box and stalls stuffed with capitalists. There you can at least hope. In the end, ma'am, I had to face the truth: the only laurels I could hope for were not for my brow, but just to souse herrings with. So I decided to go back to what I once was: a cook. And I thought to myself: the professor's daughter, Miss Helena, was so good to me in former days, why should she be different now she's a married woman? So here I am.

Helena And just at the right moment! As it happens, only yesterday I had to get rid of my maid, who proved more pleasing to my husband than to me, if you get my meaning.

Josie Impossible! How can a man have eyes for a maidservant when blessed with such a wife as you?

Helena Ah, it is obvious you know nothing about men.

Josie (*half to herself*) Oh, don't I just!

Helena (*sighing*) Those fatal pipes of Pan — I should never have listened to them. My husband has many vices.

Josie Men always have. So you've either got to stay single or take them along with the vices.

Helena Besides that, my husband is not quite up to my level intellectually. To be frank, he's rather stupid.

Josie But rich?

Helena Yes, but —

Josie Rich and stupid! What a lucky woman you are!

Helena If only — I'm doubly glad you came when you did, Josie. It's not only a servant I need, but a confidante as well. Can you start right away?

Josie Glad to, ma'am. I'm yours from now on.

Helena You see, Josie, I feel there is something mysterious going on. Stupid as my husband is, I feel he is hiding something from me.

Josie Like what?

Helena Some sort of crime perhaps.

Josie Crime!

Helena He is restless, evasive, keeps out of people's way —

Josie Yes, that sounds criminal, but —

Helena Then when he's sleeping — (*She hesitates*)

Josie Snoring?

Helena Not always, no.

Josie A lot of innocent people do that too.

Helena No, he talks. Not very distinctly, but —

Josie Like this? (*Imitating a person mumbling in sleep*) Mostly that means just, "I'm too hot".

Helena But what if it means, "If I am discovered, all is lost"? That's certainly what it sounds like to me. Josie, what if he were to have committed a murder?

Josie Madam, you're making my flesh creep! But no, it can't be that. I follow all the murders in the newspapers, and there's none just now where they don't know who did it.

As You Were

Helena I'm convinced he is hiding *some* sort of secret. And now, thank goodness, I've got you to help me discover it. Come now and help me finish my toilet. There are lots more things I have to tell you.

Helena and Josie go off L

After a while there is a knock at door C. *It is repeated, then* ——

Anthony Muffett opens the door and looks in

Muffett Nobody at home? Odd place — they advertise for servants and then are not at home to receive them. (*He enters the room. He is shabbily dressed. Looking round*) Well, it looks quite promising. Almost as good as my own was. (*He tests the sofa and easy chairs with his hands, then settles down comfortably in a chair*) Ah, quite like old times!

Hofmann, now dressed, enters R *with hat and stick*

Hofmann (*seeing Muffett*) What on earth — ?
Muffett (*springing to his feet and bowing low, so that he does not see Hofmann's face*) Your servant, sir.
Hofmann Who are you? What do you want?
Muffett (*still bowed*) To be your servant, sir. The greengrocer on the corner —
Hofmann (*laying aside hat and stick, not looking at Muffett*) Ah yes. Let's see your references. (*As he turns, hand outstretched, he recoils*) Good heavens!
Muffett (*recognizing Hofmann*) Oh, Lord! (*Turning away in dismay*) Mike, my manservant!
Hofmann (*turning away in dismay*) Mr Muffett, my former master!
Muffett (*venturing a quick look*) How he's gone up in the world!
Hofmann (*venturing a quick look*) How he's come down in the world! (*Putting up his coat collar to conceal his face*) What the devil shall I — ?

Muffett (*advancing*) You young devil, are you pretending not to know me?

Hofmann You are making a mistake. I am not the person you appear to mean.

Muffett Drop it, Mike. It's no good.

Hofmann (*with a final attempt at dignity*) Sir, I must ask you to leave the house.

Muffett As if I didn't know my own former manservant! (*In a threatening tone*) Don't try playing the fool with me, Mike.

Hofmann All right then, it's me. But please, whatever you do, no-one must —

Muffett And it seems you've become rich. If that isn't the limit! While I — Is there no justice in the world?

Hofmann (*nervously*) Please, Mr Muffett — sir — not such a noise. If my wife were to hear —

Muffett So you've got a wife, have you? And you're afraid of her? Well, that makes me feel a little better. You've got a cross to bear too.

Hofmann Excuse me — my wife is both young and beautiful.

Muffett Even worse, then. Poor devil, now I begin to feel sorry for you.

Hofmann She comes of a very good family. Her father was a professor. And she knows nothing about my former life. I made out I was a business man, a timber merchant, otherwise I should never have got her.

Muffett So you're still the fool you always were.

Hofmann There's no need to speak to me in that tone.

Muffett Since fortune turned against me I always say exactly what I think.

Hofmann What happened, then?

Muffett It's a long story. False friends, then a love affair with an actress who left me after I'd spent my all on her. Never mind that now. The point is that I am no longer a master, but a manservant — your manservant.

Hofmann You, my servant?

Muffett You're not going to throw your own former master out, are you?

As You Were

Hofmann But you can't — No, it's quite impossible.
Muffett Why? Everything's possible.
Hofmann I could never be rude to you.
Muffett Be polite then. I'm not stopping you.
Hofmann How could I ever bring myself to expect you to — well, to clean my boots?
Muffett I am not particularly eager to clean your boots. Do them yourself, or find someone else.
Hofmann And how can I take into my house somebody who once physically assaulted me?
Muffett Ah yes, I remember. I did box your ears now and again. But never mind, I'm not vindictive. It's all forgotten now.
Hofmann Not by me, it isn't. There are things one never forgets.
Muffett Such as your habit of coming home drunk on Sundays, you miserable toad.
Hofmann No, that settles it. You can't come here.
Muffett What, you wretched little upstart, you'd turn your old benefactor away from your door? Bite the hand that once fed you? Ungrateful impostor, could you have had a more magnanimous master? Did I ever count my socks or mark the wine bottles?
Hofmann I never robbed you, and don't you suggest it.
Muffett Not directly, no. You hadn't the guts to be a real criminal. But you were always forgetting to return my change, letting a few coins roll down the drain, or giving them to invisible beggars. In other words, you were a timid, indirect thief — but even that mounts up in time.
Hofmann (*going to door* C *and opening it, angrily*) Get out!
Muffett (*at door* C) Very well, if you insist, I shall go. But I may perhaps have a word or two to drop in official ears about the sort of people who are becoming timber merchants these days.
Hofmann (*holding him back as he turns to go*) No, wait a minute!
Muffett Then there are people who may be interested to know that you worked as my servant for three whole years. Not to speak of what you did with the rich banker Reichenbach.
Hofmann (*clutching him anxiously*) Look, Mr Muffett, if you really want to be my manservant, you can have the job. But you must swear never to speak one syllable —

Muffett (*shaking himself free and returning to the room*) What an ass you are!

Hofmann No, look here —

Muffett Just take care to stay in my good books, Mike, and you'll have nothing to fear. Now, what about wages? How much do I get?

Hofmann (*rather hesitantly*) I pay my servants eight pounds a week, all found.*

Muffett You miserable devil, I paid you ten.* I ought to be worth as much to you as you were to me.

Hofmann (*angrily*) That's enough now. I won't stand for any more rudeness from you. Remember who you now are.

Muffett Yes, Mike, you're right. But old habits are hard to break. I promise to be careful when we're in company.

Hofmann You'd better be. Ten pounds a week, then —

Muffett And two pounds a day for my food.

Hofmann Why that? Food is provided here.

Muffett Not what I call food. Watching you make a pig of yourself on the best of the land, while I have to make do with sausages and mash, would arouse grudges in me. If you want to be spared those you can give me two pounds right away. I'm hungry.

Hofmann I don't carry small change. (*He brings out his wallet*) I'll give you half your first week's wages in advance. (*He gives Muffett a banknote*)

Muffett There's some other things I'm in need of. So I'll take the second half now as well.

He helps himself from the open wallet Hofmann is still holding open

Hofmann No, that's going a bit too far.

Muffett Don't you trust me? (*Returning the second note to Hofmann*) All right, give it to me later. But you'll have to let me have what I want in the end, Mike, my lad, or I may find it difficult to keep my mouth shut.

Hofmann (*putting his wallet away*) Stop calling me Mike, will you?

* *See note on prelims page iii*

As You Were

Muffett That's only for when we're alone, you ass. Well, what are you waiting for? I thought you were going out?

Hofmann Yes, of course. I must find a maid for my wife. (*Taking up his hat and stick, he goes to door* C, *then looks at his watch*) Heavens, time's short. Wait here till I get back. If my wife comes in, tell her you're my new manservant. And remember to be very polite and respectful. She has very fragile nerves and wouldn't stand for the sort of language you've been using to me.

Muffett All right, I'll be careful. Now off you go.

Hofmann (*as he goes off*) Horrible fellow!

Hofmann exits

Muffett Common fellow! So rich, so stupid and so married! How disgustingly happy he'd be if his marriage hadn't come to put a damper on his heavenly bliss! If he hadn't been rich she wouldn't have married him. If he hadn't been stupid he wouldn't have married her. But as you sow, so shall you reap. Having sown richness and stupidity, he reaped the inevitable: a shrewish wife. Thus Fate lets us create our own little private hells in order to protect its own reputation as a general dispenser of justice: we get what we deserve. Pity my own outward appearance is no longer conducive to seductive approaches. Otherwise the good lady might — Well, at least one might try to arouse some preliminary interest. Why not? A slight suggestion, through bearing and facial expression, that here is a man standing on the ruins of a brilliant past; a buttoned-up manner indicating that one is above the coquettish blandishment of outward fineries. Even rags can be thus imbued with some slight sympathetic appeal (*Looking* L) Do I hear a footstep? A feminine tread, the soft swish of silk, the gentle creak of starch. She is coming, the mistress of the house.

Muffett draws back out of sight

Josie comes in R. *She is reading a newspaper that conceals her face from him*

Josie (*reading from the newspaper*) "Reichenbach's Bank Robbed, Thieves' Half-A-Million-Pound Haul". (*Lowering the newspaper, still with her back to Muffett*) It couldn't be that, could it? The mysterious crime she suspects him of?

Muffett A keen interest in criminology — that suggests a soft, romantic soul. (*He comes forward and bows low*) Madam, may I have the honour of wishing — ?

Josie (*turning quickly*) Madam? (*Regarding Muffett, who stays bowed*) Who are you?

Muffett (*still with lowered head*) Beg pardon, my lady. Your husband had graciously condescended to appoint me his personal valet.

Josie I know that voice. (*Looking closer*) Yes, it's Anthony Muffett.

Muffett (*straightening*) Good heavens, Joan of Arc!

Josie (*aside, vexedly*) Why must he come to this house of all houses? Making me ashamed —

Muffett (*tragically*) So we meet again — for the first time since those intoxicating days of old! I the man of means, reduced now to the lowly shadow of domestic serfdom, and you, the glittering stage sweetheart, the proud wife of a grovelling timber merchant. Oh Fate, you trickster!

Josie (*aside*) He thinks I'm the lady of the house. All right, I'll show him. (*Aloud to Muffett*) My dear Mr Manservant Muffett, you will surely see that in these unforeseen circumstances there can be no question of your remaining in this house.

Muffett But what if that is exactly what I do not see? Your husband has made a contract with me.

Josie Who keeps contracts nowadays? You clearly do not read the newspapers.

Muffett Vile apostle of modern practices, shame on your perfidy!

Josie Don't say such things to me, Tony. Remember who I now am. And you can also remember that my husband's grandfather was Othello's closest friend.

Muffett What's that supposed to mean? Stop blethering, Josie.

Josie He's jealous, that's what I mean. (*Coming closer*) Have a thought for my reputation.

As You Were

Muffett (*warningly*) Keep away now, please.

Josie If it became known that I once loved you — perhaps love you still — (*In melting tones, putting an arm round his neck*) Tony, for my sake, do not disturb this hallowed house.

Muffett (*momentarily succumbing*) Josie — (*Then angrily pulling away from her*) That's theatre. Shakespeare, no doubt.

Josie *A Midsummer Night's Dream.*

Muffett Don't start on me again, Josie. The play is over, and won't stand renewal.

Josie If it were to come out — I and a — well, I know things were different then, but I and a manservant —

Muffett That comes well from a woman whose present husband was once himself — (*remembering his promise*) something other than a timber merchant. You never really loved me. Now it will be my greatest delight to make things difficult — as difficult as possible for you.

Josie So you won't leave? All right, we shall see who can make the most difficulties. I have ways of getting rid of you. You'll see.

Josie goes off L

Muffett I do believe she was threatening me. Foolhardy wench, when with a few syllables I can destroy you. Your husband's past doings, your own affair with me — all so disreputable that you'll both be trembling like aspen leaves before me. Meantime, I'll keep out of sight in Mike's room. Oh, I shall serve you all right — and it will serve you right.

Muffett goes off R

After a while Helena and Josie come in L

Josie Oh, he's gone.

Helena For good, I hope. Isn't that just like my husband — to engage the first person who comes along without even consulting me?

Josie And a man who once knew better things. They always need watching.

Helena It's lucky that you recognized him.

Josie I believe there's something between them — him and your husband, I mean. Something he said, it made me feel there was some secret —

Helena You see! I was right — I felt it in my bones. He has done something criminal. I'm sure of it. Heavens, what shall I do?

Hofmann enters C

Hofmann Ah, angel wife, I've got you a new maid. She'll be here directly.

Helena It is no longer necessary. I have found one for myself.

Hofmann But you told me I must —

Helena (*indicating Josie*) Here she is.

Hofmann Well, mine wasn't bad-looking either.

Josie (*curtseying*) Your excellency.

Hofmann (*looking at her with interest, aside*) Not bad.

Josie (*aside*) I do believe he's making eyes at me.

Hofmann But what shall we do with the girl I took on?

Helena Simple: just send her away.

Hofmann Yes, of course. Though now I come to think of it, it mightn't be a bad idea to — There's enough work here for two. Let's find out which of them cooks the best, and keep the other one for the rooms.

Helena That will suit nobody.

Hofmann On the contrary, sweetheart. I —

Josie I don't want silly girls under my feet. I can cook and look after madam very well by myself. (*With a reproving look to Hofmann*) If that's what madam wants, it should be good enough for you.

Hofmann All right, all right. But there was something else I had to tell madam — I mean, you. Oh yes — I've also found a new manservant.

Helena Josie told me. You must send him away at once.

Hofmann (*exasperated*) Just a minute, angel. Do I engage people just to send them away? At least look at him first.

Helena It is not necessary.
Josie Madam doesn't like him.
Hofmann Without even seeing him?
Helena When one comes of a good family, one does not invite into one's house creatures who have come down in the world.
Hofmann But his references —
Helena — naturally fail to mention ——
Josie — that he once owned a factory ——
Helena — and then became a traveller in wines ——
Josie — or at least tried to.
Hofmann (*aside*) Confound it, they know it all!
Helena A man who in addition drops hints that he knows certain secrets which he might be tempted to reveal.
Hofmann (*aside*) So he's already been talking!
Helena (*to Josie*) Do you notice his uneasiness?
Josie Changing colour like a chameleon on a kaleidoscope. (*To Hofmann, reproachfully*) The way you treat poor madam!
Hofmann (*aside*) Now she's starting on me!
Helena Oh, my poor nerves! Come, Josie, take me to my room.
Hofmann But angel —
Helena (*shouting*) You will send him away! (*Weakly, clinging to Josie*) Or I shall go to my aunt's.
Josie (*to Hofmann*) Now look what you've done. You've no right to shout at her like that. So fine a lady must be treated gently. Come, madam.

Josie leads Helena off L

Hofmann (*bursting out once they are gone*) Saints in heaven, if she didn't come of such a disgustingly good family, I'd soon show her what nerves are. As for her new maid — And that cad Muffett has obviously been dropping hints. He must leave at once.

Muffett comes in quietly R

(*Deflated*) Oh Lord, here he comes.
Muffett What, back already?

Hofmann My business was soon settled. But you —
Muffett You want to know what I've been doing in your absence? I've been inspecting your room, and mine.
Hofmann Yours?
Muffett The room in which — I take it — your last manservant lived. A proper little dog-hole it is too. We must find something better than that for me.
Hofmann It's that or nothing. I'm sorry, but —
Muffett (*looking at him with disdainful sympathy*) It's I who feel sorry, poor chap. Your wife — daughter of a good family you said, didn't you?
Hofmann Mr Muffett, I warn you that in anything concerning my wife I will not tolerate —
Muffett It seems — particularly in regard to your wife — that you will tolerate anything.
Hofmann Sir, you leave me no alternative but to inform you that my wife has insisted on your instant dismissal.
Muffett Who else? And that empty room up there (*indicating Hofmann's head*) can do nothing but pass the message on. But I am not going. I intend to stay where I am.
Hofmann Damn it all, I've told you: my wife won't allow it, and there's an end of it.
Muffett So your wife, the pampered little professor's daughter, rejects me, does she? Now listen to me. You are a complete idiot, I know, but parts of you are good — and anyway at the moment you are my boss, so I owe you some loyalty. (*He moves closer to Hofmann*) Mike, my lad, I must tell you a thing or two, so take a hold on yourself.
Hofmann I, take a hold on myself? When, when — Upon my soul!
Muffett You see, you're trembling already. Well now, to start with: you have been deceived. Your wife is not what you think she is.
Hofmann In what way?
Muffett First of all, she's not a professor's daughter.
Hofmann Ridiculous!
Muffett I know all about her past life.
Hofmann You knew her before?

As You Were

Muffett Very well. As a matter of fact, she once, in a confidential moment, confessed to me that her father was a waiter.

Hofmann (*horrified*) A waiter!

Muffett And her mother worked in a laundry.

Hofmann Laundry!

Muffett While she herself had been in service. First as a maidservant, then as a cook.

Hofmann Cook! But this is terrible!

Muffett There's worse to come. A theatrical agent, one of those miserable secret talent spotters, decided she had possibilities as an actress and got her an engagement as a dramatic heroine.

Hofmann Oh no, Mr Muffett, I can believe much, but not that.

Muffett But if I were to tell you that she was an actress when I first met her and fell in love? We even became engaged.

Hofmann You and she?

Muffett Yes, both of us. But then she took it into her head to be unfaithful. She left me for another man. Whether it was the Italian or the Russian I don't know — they were both around at the time. Yet all the same it was me she really loved.

Hofmann You?

Muffett And, you know, I believe she still does.

Hofmann Still? No, I won't allow that.

Muffett What can you do? You can't control feelings. Oh, there are some false people in the world, you know, particularly former actresses who are now married to timber merchants. If you could have heard her, not half an hour ago, pleading with me, begging me to preserve her from your jealous wrath! If you had seen her stroking my hair, her arm around my neck! Oh, what a sight that must have been! And then —

Hofmann (*in a rage*) I shall kill you both!

Muffett Wait a moment, my friend. My behaviour, I assure you, would have rivalled the biblical Joseph, when he repulsed Potiphar's wife with the immortal words "No, on my scout's honour". You must buy me a coat of many colours, so — if it happens again — I can leave it in her hands as proof of my innocence.

Hofmann Despicable woman! But there's one thing I don't understand. What about her aunt? I mean, I know her aunt, and she's as grand as they come.

Muffett Anybody can produce an aunt, even a grand aunt. For a pound a day and a borrowed gown you can get all the aunts you want.

Hofmann But her fine manners, her education —

Muffett All put on.

Hofmann No really, this is too much! Inventing parents, hiring spurious aunts, falling in love with manservants —

Muffett Careful there, Mike. You were one yourself once.

Hofmann I shall get a divorce.

Muffett That's right. Make a clean sweep.

Josie comes in L and, seeing the two men, who do not notice her, hides behind a piece of furniture in order to listen

Hofmann I'll need you in court as a witness.

Muffett Delighted to oblige. I shall tell everything — on oath. (*Patting Hofmann's shoulder*) I shall stand by you, Mike. Never fear.

Josie (*aside*) He calls his own master "Mike"?

Hofmann But what if she starts publicly reproaching me with — you know what?

Josie (*aside*) Aha, now it's coming out.

Muffett She'll get no support from me. When it comes to keeping silent, the grave is a mother's meeting compared to me. When I remember all you did for me when you —

Hofmann (*interrupting quickly*) Don't bring that up.

Muffett And who else knows or even suspects about Reichenbach?

Hofmann For heaven's sake! If someone —

Josie (*aside*) Reichenbach! Then it *was* them who robbed the bank!

Josie hurries off L, unseen

Hofmann (*with a start*) Did you hear that?

As You Were

Muffett What?
Hofmann The door. Someone was listening!
Muffett No-one was listening. It's just your imagination. Pull yourself together, Mike. Call her in. I'll go to your room while you confront her with her past. If she denies it, ring the bell. Then I come in, like an avenging angel, to stage a modern version of the Last Trump that will differ from the original only by being played in private.

Muffett goes off R

Hofmann Yes, I shall show her up! Fine manners won't help her, nor dramatic acting. The spotlight is on me now, and I shall upstage her — you'll see!

Helena and Josie come in L. *They do not notice Hofmann at first*

Josie Be careful. He's still in the house, that man. I can feel it.
Helena It can't be true. I just cannot believe it!
Josie But I heard it with my own ears.
Hofmann (*aside*) Now for it. (*Losing courage*) Oh Lord! (*Taking a grip on himself*) Shame on you, mouse. (*Advancing, to Josie*) Leave the room. I wish to speak to my wife.
Helena Stay where you are, Josie.
Hofmann (*to Josie*) Did you hear what I said?
Josie (*backing, nervously*) For heaven's sake, your honour —
Helena What is the meaning of this?
Hofmann You'll soon know. (*To Josie*) Out!
Josie (*to Helena*) I'll see if I can find the other one.

Josie goes off R

Helena (*as Josie goes*) Be careful! (*To Hofmann*) Answer my question. Who is this man you call your —
Hofmann I want an answer from you first, professor's daughter.
Helena Later. Is this true about Reichenbach?

Hofmann (*aside*) Reichenbach! My God, she knows!

Helena Why do you start so? Why don't you speak? Did you really do that? Come, tell me.

Hofmann (*deflated*) Oh well, if you already know — Yes, I did.

Helena But why, why? (*Bursting into tears*) Oh, it's too terrible! What shall I do?

Hofmann What of it, anyway? What's so very terrible about it?

Helena What's so terrible! How can you be so brazen? And there was something else, wasn't there? Something between you and that man?

Hofmann (*crushed again*) Well, yes, that as well. (*His anger returning*) But haven't you deceived me too?

Helena I?

Hofmann The game's up, waiter's daughter! Actress! (*Advancing on her*) Now dig deep in your repertory of Ophelias and play the injured innocent all you like, it will make no difference: I am going to divorce you.

Helena Heavens, he's gone mad!

Hofmann Your mother a washerwoman!

Helena Help! Help!

Helena rushes off L

Hofmann (*shouting after her*) And who needs a new cook when you were one yourself? (*He slams the door*) That'll teach her. It's the last time I'll ever look at a professor's daughter.

Hofmann goes to the centre of the room to calm down. He has his back to the door R, *and does not see* ——

Muffett enter through it in a state of agitation

Muffett Mike, there's a limit to all things. The way your wife made a set at me!

Hofmann She knocked you over, did she? (*Chuckling*) The way she rushed out! I've never seen anybody crushed so completely flat.

As You Were

Muffett It's not very nice to be quite so openly slobbered over. And at the same time pumping me for secrets I never knew I was supposed to know.
Hofmann (*surprised*) What? When was this?
Muffett Just now.
Hofmann She must be a fast worker.
Muffett She thinks you and I played an open-sesame act with Reichenbach's safe.
Hofmann She thinks we robbed the bank? So that's why she made such a fuss! Not because —
Muffett It really is too bad. You'd think if she really thought that, she wouldn't have made such violent love to me.
Hofmann She did that?
Muffett I told you. I thought I was lost for good.
Hofmann (*angrily*) That is the last straw. Now my blood is really up.

Hofmann goes through door L *and returns at once, dragging Helena by the hand*

Come along, miserable hypocrite. Now I know the cause of all your cunning tantrums. (*He points to Muffett*) This is your secret lover.
Helena (*indignantly, snatching her hand away from him*) What are you up to now?
Muffett (*aside*) Who is this delectable duchess?
Hofmann It was to have him here in the house that you arranged —
Helena You're out of your mind.
Muffett (*to Hofmann, urgently*) Mike, you've got it all wrong. Not her! That's not the one!
Hofmann (*to Muffett*) You shut up! (*To Helena*) Do you deny being in love with this man?
Muffett Mike, what's got into you? You're losing the few brains you ever had. That's not your wife!
Hofmann What?
Muffett I don't know this lady — not a single inch of her.

Helena And I have never set eyes on this person before.

Muffett Person! There's no need to be rude, whoever you are.

Helena You are my husband's accomplice in a despicable crime. Even the word "person" is too good for you. "Villain" would be better.

Muffett (*puzzled*) You his wife?

Hofmann Who else? (*He seizes Muffett*) So you've been trying to make a fool of me, have you? All this rubbish about actresses and bank robberies! Whoever you once were, out you go!

Muffett Don't be a fool, Mike.

Hofmann (*pushing him towards door* C) And stop calling me Mike.

Muffett Remember I was once your master.

Hofmann (*stopping, embarrassed*) None of that, now.

Helena What does he mean — your master?

Muffett And once such memories begin to stir in me ——

Hofmann (*realizing defeat and releasing him with a little push*) You'd better go.

Helena What are you doing? Call the police! (*Remembering*) No don't! They'll only arrest you too.

Hofmann (*bitterly*) Would you mind? (*To Muffett*) A proper muddle you've got us into!

Helena and Muffett stand eyeing each other, unsure how to react

Josie comes in R

Josie What was all that noise about?

Muffett (*joyfully*) Josie! (*Rushing to her and pulling her forward*) This is Joan of Arc! This is the amorous secret-searcher! This is the waiter's daughter! (*To Hofmann, indicating Josie*) This is your wife.

Helena Josie?

Hofmann Our new maidservant?

Muffett Maidservant?

Josie (*to Muffett*) What have you been doing, stupid? (*To Helena*) He thought I was the master's wife. I know it was wrong of me, but when Mr Muffett came looking for a job, he took me for the lady of the house, and I couldn't resist playing along, not wanting him to see the level to which I'd been reduced since he first got to know me — and love me.

Muffett Used to, maybe.

Helena Is being my maidservant so very shameful? Look what you've done, Josie.

Hofmann Angel, sweetheart, can you forgive me?

Helena What for? Suspecting me of having a love affair, or for robbing the Reichenbach bank?

Muffett (*indicating Josie*) That's her doing too. Always making a drama out of everything. When Mike — your husband — was my manservant, I let him earn an extra penny or two sweeping the floors in Reichenbach's bank. That's all.

Helena (*to Hofmann*) Is this true? You were *his* (*indicating Muffett*) manservant?

Hofmann It's true, darling. But I never touched their money, neither his nor Reichenbach's, even when I found it lying on the floor. I was always honest, even when I was a —

Helena There is no need to tell me what you were. I found that out long ago, but forebore to mention it — out of delicacy.

Hofmann Oh my delicate, my delicious angel!

Hofmann goes to kiss her hand. She pulls her arm away

Helena And now everyone will know. How can you expect me to forgive that?

Hofmann (*piteously*) But angel —

Helena goes off L, *followed by Hofmann*

Muffett And she won't — not ever. Poor Mike! Tormenting himself for nothing. Lord, what love can do to a man! (*To Josie*) Just look what it has reduced me to!

Josie Or me. Servants, both of us. (*Satirically*) Yes, ma'am, your bath is ready, ma'am.

Muffett (*likewise*) The blue suit, sir? As you please, sir.

Laughing, they embrace

Oh Josie, the relief of knowing you are not his wife, you've no idea! I should never have let you go. Let's try again, shall we?
Josie Not here. If she forgives him, she'll never forgive me. (*Mimicking Helena*) "Is being my maidservant so very shameful?" Did you see her face? We're both out of a job.
Muffett Never mind, we'll start again, rebuild things together. What's the soldiers' command when they know they've made a mistake? "As you were" — yes, that's it.
Josie As you were, then. So, let's not stand on the order of our going, but go at once.
Muffett Shakespeare?
Josie Near enough.

Hand in hand they go off C

The stage is empty for a moment, then Hofmann comes in L, *followed by Helena*

Hofmann Ha, it seems they've gone.
Helena Which means that again we have no servants. And it's all your fault. Whatever possessed you to engage that impossible man?
Hofmann And who was to blame for the impossible woman?
Helena Yes, well you'd better stop arguing and start looking for replacements.
Hofmann I have found one for you. I told you. She'll be here any minute now.
Helena If you chose her, I probably won't like her. So find a few alternatives. And at once, otherwise I'll go—
Helena } (*simultaneously*) { — to my aunt's.
Hofmann } { — to your aunt's.
I must say, my angel, you are a very disagreeable angel this morning.

On this echo of the squabble with which the play began the CURTAIN *falls*

FURNITURE AND PROPERTY LIST

Further dressing may be added at the director's discretion

Off stage: Newspaper (**Josie**)

Personal: **Hofmann**: watch, wallet. *In it*: banknotes

LIGHTING PLOT

Property fittings required: nil
Interior. The same throughout

To open: Overall general lighting

No cues

EFFECTS PLOT

No cues